Energy for Today

Solar Power

By Tea Benduhn

Reading consultant: Susan Nations, M.Ed.,
author/literacy coach/consultant in literacy development

Science and curriculum consultant: Debra Voege, M.A.,
science curriculum resource teacher

WEEKLY READER®
PUBLISHING

Please visit our web site at www.garethstevens.com.
For a free color catalog describing our list of high-quality books,
call 1-800-542-2595 (USA) or 1-800-387-3178 (Canada). Our fax: 1-877-542-2596

Library of Congress Cataloging-in-Publication Data

Benduhn, Tea.
    Solar power / by Tea Benduhn.
        p. cm. — (Energy for today)
    Includes bibliographical references and index.
    ISBN-10: 0-8368-9263-1 — ISBN-13: 978-0-8368-9263-5 (lib. bdg.)
    ISBN-10: 0-8368-9362-X — ISBN-13: 978-0-8368-9362-5 (softcover)
    1. Photovoltaic power systems—Juvenile literature.   2. Solar power plants—Juvenile literature.
    I. Title.
  TK1087.B466   2009
  621.47—dc22   2008015515

This edition first published in 2009 by
Weekly Reader® Books
An Imprint of Gareth Stevens Publishing
1 Reader's Digest Road
Pleasantville, NY 10570-7000 USA

Copyright © 2009 by Gareth Stevens, Inc.

Senior Managing Editor: Lisa M. Herrington
Senior Editor: Brian Fitzgerald
Creative Director: Lisa Donovan
Designer: Ken Crossland
Photo Researcher: Diane Laska-Swanke
Special thanks to Kirsten Weir

Image credits: Cover and title page: © Russell Illig/Getty Images; p. 5: © Triff/Shutterstock; p. 6: © Ariel Skelley/
Blend Images/Jupiter Images; p. 7: © Andrew Lambert Photography/Photo Researchers, Inc.; p. 9: © Leigh Haeger/
Weekly Reader; p. 10: © Peter Essick/Aurora/Getty Images; pp. 11 (both), 20: NASA; p. 12: © Yvan/Shutterstock;
p. 13: © NASA/Getty Images; p. 15: © Peter Menzel/Photo Researchers, Inc.; p. 16: © Otmar Smit/Shutterstock;
p. 18: © Florian Schulz/Alamy; p. 19: © Stefano Paltera/American Solar/Getty Images; p. 21: © Elena Elisseeva/
Shutterstock.

Printed in the United States

1 2 3 4 5 6 7 8 9 10 09 08

Table of Contents

Words that appear in the glossary are printed in **boldface** type the first time they occur in the text.

Chapter 1

What Is Solar Power?

At night, stars twinkle in the sky. During the day, one star shines in the sky. That star is our Sun. It is the center of our **solar system**. The solar system contains the Sun and the planets that **orbit**, or circle, it. The Sun is more than one hundred times bigger than Earth! The Sun is an important source of **energy**. All living things need the Sun's energy.

The Sun gives off heat and light. Both heat and light are kinds of energy.

We could not see without sunlight. The Sun's heat keeps Earth at the right temperature. Even in winter, the Sun keeps Earth warm enough for life. Heat from the Sun helps create wind and causes our weather. The Sun's heat and light give plants and animals energy to grow and move. The use of the Sun's light and heat energy is called solar power.

Plants need energy from the Sun to grow. Plants take in heat energy and light energy from the Sun. They store some of that energy inside them. Some plants, such as corn, are food. When we eat plants, we take in their stored energy. The energy from the Sun moves from plants to people. The food is our fuel. It gives us energy to play or do schoolwork.

Energy from the Sun is stored in the food we eat. The food gives us energy to play.

Solar-powered calculators run on energy from sunlight.

The Sun's energy can also power machines. You may have used a solar-powered calculator in math class, for example. Solar calculators do not need batteries. Instead, they collect energy from light! Solar energy can power bigger machines, too. We can use solar power to make electricity. Electricity powers the lights and computers in our schools and homes.

Chapter 2

Sources of Energy

Like all stars, the Sun is a huge ball of hot gas. Deep inside the Sun, gases explode. They release huge amounts of light and heat. If we could collect an hour's worth of sunlight hitting Earth, we would have enough energy to power all the buildings in the world for a whole year.

The Greenhouse Effect

Some heat escapes into space.

Most heat is trapped in the atmosphere.

Sun

Heat from the Sun hits Earth.

Earth

Atmosphere

How does the Sun warm Earth? Imagine plants growing inside a greenhouse. The greenhouse has walls made of glass. Heat and light from the Sun enter the greenhouse and get trapped inside. The gases in Earth's **atmosphere** work like a greenhouse. The gases trap heat from the Sun close to Earth. This is called the **greenhouse effect**. It helps keep Earth warm enough for us to live.

A power plant burns coal to make electricity. Coal is a fossil fuel.

Most of our energy does not come from the Sun. Today, we get most of our energy from **fossil fuels**. Oil, gas, and coal are fossil fuels. They are made from the remains of plants and animals that died long ago. Burning oil, gas, and coal gives off energy. We use fossil fuels to make gasoline and electricity.

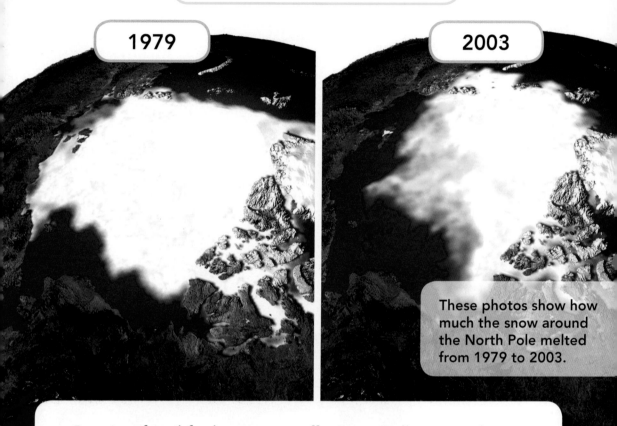

Polar Ice Caps

1979

2003

These photos show how much the snow around the North Pole melted from 1979 to 2003.

Burning fossil fuels causes **pollution**. Pollution makes the air dirty and hard to breathe. Burning fossil fuels also releases gases that are making Earth slowly heat up. This rise in temperature is called **global warming**. Scientists say global warming may cause the ice to melt at the North and South poles. The melted ice could cause sea levels to rise.

Today, people are burning more fossil fuels than ever before. Greenhouse gases from fossil fuels are making global warming happen faster. There is another problem with using fossil fuels. We are starting to run out of them. Fossil fuels are **nonrenewable resources**. After fossil fuels are used up, they are gone forever.

Oil rigs drill for fossil fuels deep under the ocean floor. When we burn fossil fuels for energy, they cannot be replaced.

Every minute of every day, the Sun i shining somewhere on Earth.

   Unlike fossil fuels, the Sun is a **renewable resource**. We will never run out of sunlight. The Sun shines all the time. Even at night or on a cloudy day, the Sun is shining somewhere on Earth. If we used more solar power for energy, we could use less fossil fuels. This would keep the air cleaner and slow global warming.

Chapter 3

How Solar Power Works

People have always used the Sun's power. Solar ovens use the Sun's heat to cook food. For centuries, people have also built houses to use the Sun's energy. Some houses have windows that face south to collect the most sunlight. Some have thick walls that soak up the Sun's heat during the day. At night, the walls let off the heat and keep people warm.

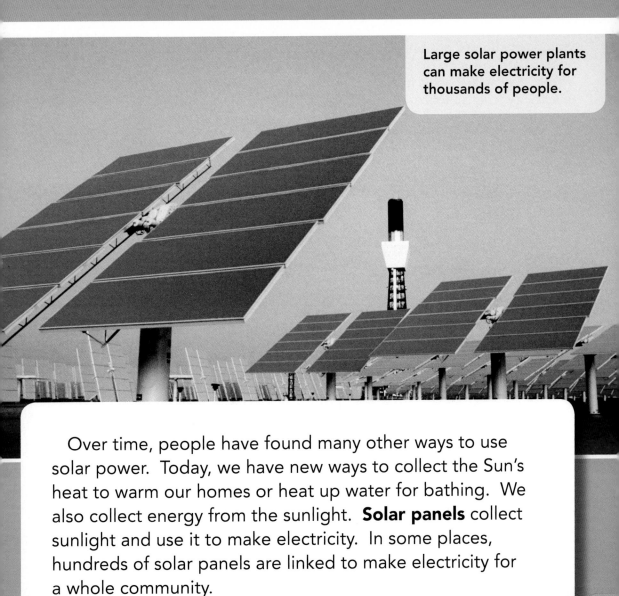

Large solar power plants can make electricity for thousands of people.

Over time, people have found many other ways to use solar power. Today, we have new ways to collect the Sun's heat to warm our homes or heat up water for bathing. We also collect energy from the sunlight. **Solar panels** collect sunlight and use it to make electricity. In some places, hundreds of solar panels are linked to make electricity for a whole community.

Some new homes are built with solar panels on their roofs. The solar panels make electricity from sunlight.

Today, many homes and buildings have solar panels on their roofs. Solar power works best in places that are hot and sunny all year. What happens when the Sun is not shining? The solar panels are connected to a battery. The battery stores electricity made by the panels. When it is dark or cloudy, people use the electricity stored in the battery.

Chapter 4

Solar Power in the Future

Solar power is a clean, renewable energy source. Yet in the United States, we get less than 1 percent of our energy from solar power. Solar panels are expensive. After a solar panel is built, however, the energy it collects from the Sun is free!

Campers can use special solar panels for electricity. The Army uses tents that have solar panels woven right into them!

Scientists are working on ways to make solar panels less expensive. They are trying to make solar panels smaller and more powerful, too. They have already invented a type of solar fabric. Solar fabric has very tiny solar panels woven into it. The Army uses solar fabric to make tents. The tents can power computers!

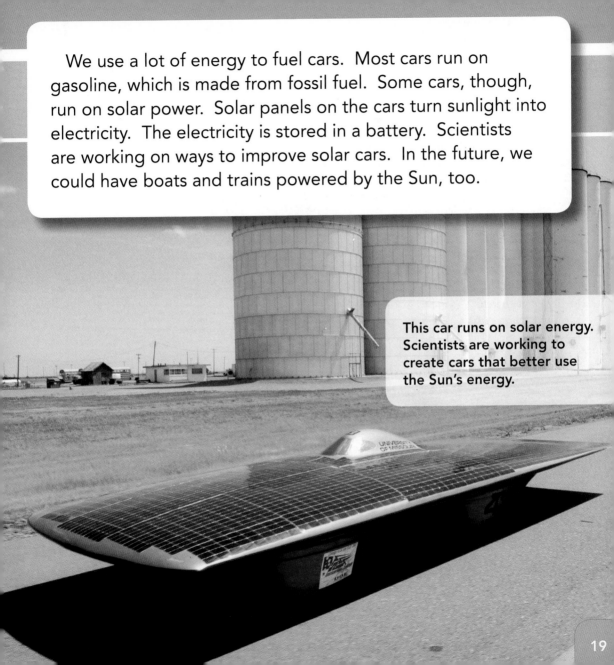

We use a lot of energy to fuel cars. Most cars run on gasoline, which is made from fossil fuel. Some cars, though, run on solar power. Solar panels on the cars turn sunlight into electricity. The electricity is stored in a battery. Scientists are working on ways to improve solar cars. In the future, we could have boats and trains powered by the Sun, too.

This car runs on solar energy. Scientists are working to create cars that better use the Sun's energy.

Solar panels

The International Space Station runs on the Sun's power. The station is a large research lab in space.

Sunlight also powers vehicles beyond Earth! Sunlight is strong in space. Solar-powered space vehicles have traveled on Mars. The International Space Station also runs on solar power. Some scientists want to build solar power plants in space, or even on the Moon. **Satellites** would collect solar energy there and send it to Earth.

Scientists are always looking for more ways to use the Sun's energy. We must also find ways to **conserve**, or save, energy. How can you use less energy? You might read near a sunny window instead of turning on a lamp. The Sun is a great source of energy. Let's use it!

You can save energy by turning off the lights when you are not using them. Go outside and use sunlight instead!

Glossary

atmosphere: the thick layer of air that surrounds Earth

conserve: to save

energy: the ability to do work

fossil fuels: sources of energy, such as oil, gas, and coal, that formed from the remains of plants or animals that lived millions of years ago

global warming: the slow rise in Earth's temperature

greenhouse effect: the warming of Earth's surface by trapping the Sun's light and heat

nonrenewable resource: a resource that cannot be used again. Once it is used, it is gone forever. Fossil fuels are nonrenewable resources.

orbit: to move around an object in a circular path

pollution: harmful materials in the environment

renewable resource: a resource that can be used again. Renewable resources include air, water, sunlight, wind, and plants and animals.

satellites: spacecraft that orbit planets or moons

solar panels: devices that collect energy from the Sun

solar system: the Sun and the planets and other space objects that orbit it

To Find Out More

Books

Harnessing Power from the Sun. Energy Revolution (series). Niki Walker (Crabtree, 2007)

Solar Power. Sources of Energy (series). Diane Gibson (Smart Apple Media, 2004)

The Sun. In the Sky (series). Carol Ryback (Weekly Reader Books, 2006)

Web Sites

Kaboom! Energy

tiki.oneworld.net/energy/energy.html

Find out about many sources of energy, including solar power.

Roofus' Solar & Efficient Home

www1.eere.energy.gov/kids/roofus

Take a tour of a home in which all the appliances—and the car—run on solar power.

Publisher's note to educators and parents: Our editors have carefully reviewed these web sites to ensure that they are suitable for children. Many web sites change frequently, however, and we cannot guarantee that a site's future contents will continue to meet our high standards of quality and educational value. Be advised that children should be closely supervised whenever they access the Internet.

Index

About the Author

Tea Benduhn writes books and edits a magazine. She lives in the beautiful state of Wisconsin with her husband and two cats. The walls of their home are lined with bookshelves filled with books. Tea says, "I read every day. It is more fun than watching television!"